THEPOETICUNDERGROUND

reverie

ISBN 978-1-291-69215-0

thepoeticunderground.tumblr.com

ISBN 978-1-291-69215-0

For every single person who has supported
me and sent me encouragement
over the past two years:
I am eternally grateful.

thepoeticunderground.tumblr.com

CONTENTS

The Storyteller   6

Beauty   7

Arrow   8

Chance   10

Beautiful   11

Bones   12

Sweater   14

For You   15

Dark   16

Exist   18

Greener Grass   19

Homesick   20

Demons   22

Hands and Feet   23

My Mind Is An Overgrown Jungle   24

Hide And Seek   26

If I Could Sing   27

Pain   28

Just Words   30

Never Trust A Mirror   31

Love Letters   32

Monsters   34

Scars   35

I Believe   36

Scars and Bruises   38

Mountains   39

Now   41

Once Upon A Time   42

Paths   43

Ribbons   45

Right Write   47
Seven   48
Teeth   49
Masked   51
Roses   52
A Poem For Society   53
Run   56
Seaside   57
Empty Spaces   58
Sadness   60
Sticks and Stones   61
The Wading Pool   62
She & He   64
Somebody   67
Talent   68
The Thing About Sadness   70
Universe   71
View   72
Gripped   74
Trapped   75
Welcome To Society   76
This   78
Breakdown   79
Okay   80
Stars   82
The Writer   83

The Storyteller

She has a bookshelf for a heart,
And ink runs through her veins,
She'll write you into her story,
With the typewriter in her brain,
Her bookshelf 's getting crowded,
With all the stories that she's penned,
Of the people who flicked through her pages,
But closed the book before the end,
And there's one pushed to the very back,
That sits collecting dust,
With its title in her finest writing,
"The One's Who Lost My Trust",
There's books she's scared to open,
And books she doesn't close,
Stories of every person she's met,
Stretched out in endless rows,
Some people have only a sentence,
While others once held a main part,
Thousands of inky footprints,
That they've left across her heart,
You might wonder why she does this,
Why write of people she once knew?
But she hopes one day she'll mean enough,
For someone to write about her too.

~e.h

Beauty

If one of the things you believe in,
Is that this world's an ugly place,
You must have never gone outside at night,
And stared up into space,
You haven't felt the way the air changes,
In the minutes before it rains,
Or watched the world pass by below,
Out the window of a plane,
You've never been awake so early,
That you see the moment the sun starts to rise,
And you've never lain with your back on the grass,
And made shapes with the clouds in the sky,
But maybe if you've done all this,
But still don't believe it's not true,
It's because you can't see all the beauty,
That I see when I look at you.

~e.h

Arrow

I made my life an arrow,
The tip a deadly sharpened point,
So people never came so close,
That I may disappoint,
I'd sit and watch in silence,
As the world would pass me by,
Wondering how far I'd fall,
If I ever tried to fly,
You watched me with such interest,
Like it was me you'd tried to find,
As though you knew all of my secrets,
And the thoughts within my mind,
You looked like all the others,
But what I did not know;
Was while I'd made myself an arrow,
You had made yourself a bow,
And apart we'd both been useless,
But we'd finally worked out why,
Since you need someone to pull you back,
If you ever want to fly,
So you aimed me with precision,
And I flew straight from the start,
Until I landed with a solid thud,
On the target of your heart.

~e.h

They say you're never really alone,
And I suppose that's sort of true,
But my shadow isn't much company,
When I'm wishing it was you.

~e.h

Chance

If you looked in the corners,
You'd find her right there,
Hidden by darkness,
And the curls in her hair,
Her nose in a book,
With her head in the clouds,
Hiding her feelings,
Away from the crowds,
If you sat by her side,
While the world passed you by
She'd tell you the story,
Behind the pain in her eyes,
If you gave her five minutes,
You'd see how her smile,
Makes even the bad things
In life seem worthwhile,
But you don't look in corners,
You don't even glance,
So she sits there still waiting,
To be given a chance.

~e.h

Beautiful

You see something that's beautiful,
So unfettered and so free,
And you yearn to know the secret,
Behind possessing such beauty,
So you catch it in your netting,
And you pin it to the ground,
Then poke and prod for hours,
Until its secret has been found,
You examine it so closely,
Always wanting something more,
Until you slowly start to notice,
Its golden blood across the floor,
You rush to find its heartbeat,
But find silence in its place,
And a realisation hits you,
As tears slip down your face,
That the secret wasn't hidden,
Because it wasn't there at all,
It was the simple act of living,
That had you so enthralled,
That you'd spent your whole life waiting,
For your beauty to be shown,
But in wanting someone else's,
You had failed to see your own.

~e.h

Bones

If you peered in through her ribcage,
You'd find an empty space,
From the boy she gave her heart to,
Who didn't put his in its place,
She no longer is the owner,
Of the blood within her veins,
It belongs to all the memories,
And the drugs to numb the pain,
The brain within her skull,
Is so flooded it could drown,
In names of people who said they cared,
But didn't stick around,
All the words that she's been called,
Have replaced all of her bones,
Even the smile upon her lips,
Is no longer her own,
There's nothing left of her body,
That society hasn't touched,
Yet they have the nerve to wonder why,
She hates herself so much.

~e.h

You warned me not to love,
That you just weren't worth my time,
But your flaws are only fatal,
Because I'd kill to make them mine.

~e.h

Sweater

You're like my favourite sweater,
That smells of places it has been,
With my tears caught in its fabric,
And my life sewn in its seams,
It's seen its share of sunshine,
And it's kept me warm in snow,
Its bright colours now a memory,
Of a time lost long ago,
But like my favourite sweater,
You've been worn out once too much,
And the stitches that protect you,
Start to crumble with my touch,
I've even tried to fix you,
But I never learnt to sew,
And the only thing that's left to do,
Is learn to let you go,
My old and worn out sweater,
It no longer fits me snug,
It's as loose as your two arms were,
The last time we ever hugged,
So promise me just one thing,
As I bid you both farewell,
That you remember me long after,
My favourite sweater's lost my smell.

~e.h

14

For You

I wish that I could hold your heart,
Cradle it gently in my hands,
But my arms just are not strong enough,
To hold what I don't understand,
My eyes have seen a lot of things,
And I thought I'd seen them all,
But the way your smile ignites my own,
Makes me think there's so much more,
These walls around this heart of mine,
Have stood collecting dust,
But it's as though you've found the gate,
That leads right to my trust,
I've never really liked my name,
But on your lips it sounds so sweet,
And your voice is my new favourite song,
That's forever on repeat,
But even though I feel all this,
I can never let you see,
Because your heart deserves a whole lot more,
Than a broken girl like me.

~e.h

Dark

Her story's written on her skin,
An artwork of her pain,
She tells herself the art's complete,
But keeps adding lines again,
She locks herself up in her room,
The blade her only friend,
Waiting for the day to come,
When her scars would start to mend,
The world around her doesn't care,
All the people carry on,
Not noticing she isn't there,
That her will for life is gone,
But there comes a single shining light,
That marks the tunnels end,
This light is made of people,
Of her family and friends,
They pull her from the hole she's in,
And provide much needed hope,
Give her joy in life again,
And teach her how to cope,
Although her scars are yet to fade,
She knows until they do,
She'll keep them as a reminder,
Of the times she's made it through.

-e.h

We all have holes right through our hearts,
I'm sure you've got them too,
But it's funny how the hole in mine,
Is shaped a lot like you.

~e.h

Exist

So many people walk this earth,
With purpose in their eyes,
But in their heart of hearts they know,
What they're living is a lie,
The alarm goes off at 6am,
Like every other day,
So they can walk into a job they hate,
Because they need the pay,
All time does is take from them,
But it never seems to give,
Always waiting for the day to come,
When they finally start to live,
I'm all too scared that one day soon,
I'll become just like the rest,
Only walking with the crowd,
Because my dreams have been oppressed,
That one day I'll look back on life,
At the opportunities that I missed,
And realise I never truly lived,
All I did was just exist.

~e.h

Greener Grass

What if grass is greener on the other side,
Because it's always raining there,
Where the ones who never fail to give,
Hardly have enough to spare,
Where the people with the broadest smiles,
Have pillows filled with tears,
And the bravest ones you've ever known,
Are crippled by their fears,
It's filled with lonely people,
But they're never seen alone,
Where those that lack real shelter,
Make you feel the most at home,
Maybe their grass looks greener,
Because they've painted on its hue,
Just remember from the other side,
Your grass looks greener too.

~e.h

Homesick

I'm homesick for places I haven't yet been,
My eyes crave the beauty of sights I've not seen,
Places unpronounceable are calling my name,
A fire I can't see warms me with its flame,
My feet walk the same path when I leave and come back,
Where once there was nothing I've worn down a track,
And my ears they get tired of the same boring tune,
Where streetlights are so bright I can't see the moon,
I'm homesick for places away from my own,
Where the people are friendly and my name is not known,
You can tell me I'm crazy but I'll never forget,
I'm homesick for places I haven't been yet.

~e.h

I promise I will save you,
When you cannot stay afloat,
And if your tears can fill an ocean,
Then for you I'll be a boat.

~e.h

Demons

There's a demon living in my head,
But she answers to my name,
She tells me stories late at night,
That are messing with my brain,
When I stand before a mirror,
She laughs at what I wear,
The freckles sprinkled on my face,
And the way I tie my hair,
Do the people sitting on the train,
Fight these demons too?
The kind that make you doubt yourself,
And tell you what to do,
Maybe that's why they never talk,
Because they're screaming in their head,
Why would you hate someone else,
When you can hate yourself instead?

~e.h

Hands and Feet

Day after day,
I walk the same streets,
Waiting for a moment,
When somebody's feet,
Stop traversing the sidewalk,
And simply stand,
Beside my lone figure,
And reach for my hand,
A gesture so simple,
Yet so hard to do,
To stick to the promise,
Of "I'll be here for you",
We don't fight the same battles,
But we fight the same war,
And I'll give you my trust,
If you give me yours,
For as long as this world,
Keeps coming untied,
I'll be there to fix it,
Right by your side,
But no feet stop walking,
They all have somewhere to be,
Until the only ones left,
Are my shadow and me.

~e.h

My Mind Is An Overgrown Jungle

My mind is an overgrown jungle,
And your axe blade won't help you at all,
Because the vines of my pain are too thick here,
And the thorns of my sorrow too tall,
My mind is an overgrown jungle,
There's no entrance to let you inside,
In fear that you'll cut down my branches,
And find the feelings I've worked hard to hide,
The vines tie in knots in my jungle,
To form a rooftop that blocks out the light,
So the sun might be warm on the outside,
But the inside's as cold as the night,
There's a house made of thorns in my jungle,
I've spent years making it feel like home,
I can do anything that I want here,
To take my mind off the fact I'm alone,
Because the problem with overgrown jungles,
Is there's always more vines that will sprout,
And I know that it's hard to get in here,
But it's ten times as hard to get out.

~e.h

Don't ever think you're alone here,
We've just been trapped in different hells,
And people aren't against you dear,
They're just all for themselves.

~e.h

Hide and Seek

When you were young you played hide and go seek,
You'd run away as they counted to ten,
Slot yourself into the smallest of places,
And wait to be found once again,
You could play this game for hours,
Since each new turn was such a thrill,
Knowing that you could escape from the world,
If only you kept yourself still,
But the thing about playing hide and go seek,
Is you got so good at the game,
That you found yourself hiding in everyday life,
Blocking your ears as the world called your name,
All the people you left are the seekers,
Yet are unaware that you need to be found,
How could anyone know that you're hidden,
When they forget you're no longer around?
But in a world with billions of people,
There's bound to be someone like you,
Someone who's playing their very own game,
Hiding in the places you like to hide too,
And one day they'll look in your corner,
Where no one has looked before,
And they'll make you forget all the reasons why,
You've even been hiding at all.

~e.h

If I Could Sing

If I could sing I'd sing you a song,
With all the words I should have said,
And I'd write it on the backs of the envelopes,
Of all your letters I still haven't read,
If I could sing I'd sing you the story,
Of how my eyes went to you in a crowd,
And I'd end it with the apology,
I was too scared to say out loud,
But I know that I'm not good at singing,
Because it was the one thing on which we agreed,
So now all the words that you wanted to hear,
Are written down in a poem you won't read.

~e.h

Pain

If I showed you my teardrops,
Would you collect them like rain,
Store them in jars,
That are labeled with "Pain",
Would you follow their tracks,
From my eyes down my cheeks,
As they write all the stories,
I'm too scared to speak,
Would you stop them with kisses,
Bring their flow to a halt,
As you teach me that pain,
Isn't always my fault,
Would you hold my face gently,
As you dry both my eyes,
And whisper the words,
"You're too precious to cry",
If I showed you my teardrops,
Would you show me your own,
And learn though we're lonely,
We're never alone.

~e.h

Let me be your one,
Let me be your only,
Let me be the only thing,
That stops you feeling lonely.

~e.h

Just Words

Are they really "just words" strung out across paper,
Or are they answers to questions we've not learnt to ask,
If they're really "just words" then how come when we read them,
We feel like somebody has seen through our mask,
I don't think "just words" can hold such a power,
That makes us believe that there really is hope,
There has to be something in words that will help you,
Hold on when you're reaching the end of your rope,
The people that write them are dealing with magic,
They change the whole world with a paper and pen,
And that I may be one is a dream I'd keep having,
If given the chance to live my life again,
They can't be "just words" when you stop feeling lonely,
As if the author is someone that you've always known,
Like a hand has reached out to brush tears from your cheek,
When you're reading the words in your room all alone.

~e.h

Never Trust a Mirror

Never trust a mirror,
For a mirror always lies,
It makes you think that all you're worth,
Can be seen from the outside.
Never trust a mirror,
It only shows you what's skin deep,
You can't see how your eyelids flutter,
When you're drifting off to sleep,
It doesn't show you what the world sees,
When you're only being you,
Or how your eyes just light up,
When you're loving what you do,
It doesn't capture when you're smiling,
Where no one else can see,
And your reflection cannot tell you,
Everything you mean to me,
Never trust a mirror,
For it only shows your skin,
And if you think that it dictates your worth,
It's time you looked within.

~e.h

Love Letters

I'd write love letters to the earth,
Whisper them to the wind,
Fold them into paper boats,
And find a stream to sail them in,
I'd write of beautiful sunrises,
Of the oranges and pinks,
While I sit beside the seashore,
Where the waves can smudge my ink,
I'd write these words on paper,
But for paper I need trees,
Like many things mankind has made,
But doesn't really need,
And so our letters to the earth,
Leave less love than they do scars,
When we write them in our blinding light,
That blocks out all the stars,
So when writing letters to the earth,
It's time that we rethink,
Since we don't need a piece of paper,
If the life we live's the ink.

~e.h

Such a curse is constant beauty,
When it surrounds us every day,
We whine that we can't see the forest,
For the trees are in the way.

~e.h

Monsters

I need a nightlight for my head,
For that's where the monsters hide,
They once were all beneath my bed,
But now they're all inside,
I hear them moving in my brain,
They won't let my thoughts be still,
They're immune to all my treatments,
All the medicines and pills,
I try to make them go to sleep,
When I lie down for the night,
But it's their favourite time to stomp around,
They won't turn off the light,
They find most joy in sorting,
My memories from years ago,
The ones I'd carefully stored away,
In a box of 'Things I wish I didn't know',
These monsters up inside my head,
Will never really leave,
Until they dig up all the memories,
They're able to retrieve,
So I guess that I could fight them,
Or I could listen while they teach,
That the memories we can learn from most,
Are the ones placed out of reach,
These monsters can get tiring,
But they keep me company in my head,
And I think my thoughts would get lonely,
If they lived under my bed.

~e.h

Scars

The teardrops run down,
And fall off of her nose,
She cries in dark corners,
Where nobody goes,
You can follow the tracks,
From her eyes to her chin,
Years upon years,
Of letting them win,
And her eyes tell a story,
Of anger and pain,
You think that she's happy,
But just look again,
And the scars of her past,
Hidden under her clothes,
Are a roadmap to places,
That nobody knows,
Her smile is now painted,
She's a master of disguise,
And you can see it all,
Just look into her eyes.

~e.h

I Believe

I believe in trusting myself,
When they all say I am wrong,
I believe in hiding my pain,
And always staying strong,
I believe the ones you trust,
Are the ones that tear you down,
I believe that always smiling,
Makes you forget the need to frown,
I believe in the little things,
The flowers and the breeze,
I believe the weakest people,
Are ones that beg upon their knees,
I believe that broken trust,
Is the reason there is hate,
I believe in perfect timing,
Never early, never late,
I believe in many things,
And the reason that I do,
Is if I believe something,
Maybe it'll believe in me too.

~e.h

If I could tell you only one thing,
My message would be this;
The world would be a lonely place,
If you did not exist.

~e.h

Scars and Bruises

This universe has a language,
That the world we live in uses,
But it's not made of twenty-six letters,
It's made of scars and bruises,
It doesn't write its words on paper,
It writes upon our skin,
So many dots and dashes,
That we can't tell where they begin,
We don't understand this language,
That the world we live in speaks,
So we mistake its poems and proses,
As a sign of being weak,
We hate our scars and bruises,
Hide them away so no-one sees,
Instead of stating proudly,
"Look what the world wrote just for me",
A lot of scars and bruises,
Will slowly fade away,
But there will always be those special few,
That the world made sure would stay,
Savour these scars and bruises,
For if you wait for enough time,
You'll find someone with the faith and love,
To decipher every line.

~e.h

Mountains

He knows their love is worth the climb,
But she's afraid of heights,
And her crooked smile is as perfect,
As the holes ripped in her tights,
Every time they're at the sea,
The oceans start to weep,
Wishing they were half as wide,
As his love for her is deep,
He tries to tell her every day,
That the words he speaks are true,
But her heart just isn't strong enough,
To say, "I love you too",
So when he climbed the mountains peak,
He found himself alone,
And that the view is lovely from the top,
But it's worthless on your own.

~e.h

You can take off all the clothes you wore,
But you can't take off regret,
You can block your ears from hearing more,
But you can't make your mind forget.

~e.h

Now

We're waiting for tomorrow,
But tomorrow never comes,
Our last breath is right upon our heels,
Yet we still refuse to run,
86 400 seconds,
And we're in another day,
All slipping through our fingers,
As we look the other way,
Days, weeks, months and years,
Are made up of right now,
A string of fleeting moments,
That we never can pin down,
We gaze into the future,
As though it's where we're meant to be
Always planning for that day,
When we can say that we're happy,
We spend so long looking forward,
That we may as well be blind,
Since we don't see until the very end,
All the things we've left behind,
Now I know it's just a theory,
But I think I've worked out how,
The only way to happiness,
Is to love what we have now.

~e.h

Once Upon a Time

What if I read to you a story,
Starting; "Once Upon A Time",
And you realised that it was your life,
Spelt out on every line,
Would you hear my voice with wonder,
As it brushed across each word,
And pray my arms had strength to hold,
The truth about your world,
Would your view on life be different,
And would it shock you most to find,
That the things you thought defined you,
Could be summed up in just two lines,
And all the ones you took for granted,
The ins and outs of every day,
Play a bigger part in who you are,
Than you'd ever dared to say,
Would you wonder at the pages left,
And all the places that they'll lead,
Then vow to make each moment,
One that you'd be proud to read,
Because there is a story of your life,
But it's you that holds the pen,
And I hope you fill the pages right,
Before you reach the end.

~e.h

Paths

From the second that you're in this world,
They tell you what is "fair",
The questions you're allowed to ask,
And the ones you wouldn't dare,
Placed on the path they've paved for you,
Life pushes you along,
Without the chance to stop and think,
If it's right where you belong,
But beyond your pathway's edges,
Is where living really starts,
A land of risks and danger,
And a land of broken hearts,
They'll tell you you should fear this land,
That there's no good there at all,
As they live their lives as they've been taught,
Behind expectation's wall,
But the best people you will ever meet,
Have wandered off their track,
Found themselves along the way,
And have no need to wander back,
So forget about life's road map,
Follow your heart at any cost,
For you'll never truly find yourself,
If you're too scared to get lost.

~e.h

They tell you to never look back,
To be afraid of what you would find,
But maybe they just don't want you to know,
What you're running from's all in your mind.

~e.h

Ribbons

She swings upon the playground,
Bright blue ribbons in her hair,
And the kids tell her that she's weird,
But she doesn't really care,
She goes home to her mother,
Who asks about her day,
She's happy being six years old,
Since there's always time to play.

She looks out at the playground,
From her cold and hard school chair,
And the kids all call her crazy,
And rip the ribbons from her hair,
She goes home to her mother,
But she doesn't ask about her day,
She doesn't enjoy being ten,
Because there isn't time to play.

Her new school has no playground,
And the kids have learned to swear,
They tell her she's a waste of space,
And she decides to cut her hair,
She goes home to her mother,
But she's working late instead,
She wishes she wasn't fifteen,
And that she could just be dead.

She drives to her old playground,
And sits on the swings seat.
Before she sees a bright blue ribbon,
Lying crumpled at her feet.
She'd go home to her mother,
But she no longer lives there,
Being eighteen is a lot of work,
When there's nobody who cares.

She's learnt to hate all playgrounds,
Since the sight fills her with dread,
And the voices of the children,
Come flooding back into her head,
She wishes she could go back,
To when she didn't care.
Where the only things that came untied.
Were the ribbons in her hair,

~e.h

Right Write

When I was only five years old,
I loved to read and write,
Stories of fairies and dragons,
And dolls come alive in the night.
When I was in the first grade,
I wrote fantasies galore,
And my mother was so proud of me,
They found a home on our fridge door.
When I was in the seventh grade,
The books were all assigned,
And my mother never read my stories,
Because she didn't have the time,
Then when I had reached grade ten,
My teacher pulled me to the side,
Told me to stop writing fiction,
And handed me an essay guide.
I didn't bring my essays home,
And I never showed my mum,
I stopped writing all together,
Because I didn't find it fun,
Now school's supposed to teach you,
But it only taught me I was wrong,
And I sure would like to write again,
But my imagination's gone.

~e.h

Seven

If I met my seven year old self today,
What would I tell her,
What would I say?
Would I warn her of the future,
Of the bad things yet to come?
Or would I leave her be naive,
To keep having fun?
Because my seven year old self,
Believed the world a perfect place,
Would she recognise herself,
When she looked into my face?
Even though I've learnt so much more,
And ten years have passed since then,
I would give up everything I have,
To view life through her eyes again.

~e.h

Teeth

The day I lost my very first tooth,
Was halfway through grade four,
I'd run my tongue along the gap,
Where my tooth had been before,
I remember I went home crying,
And showed it to my mum,
She told me that a brand new tooth,
Would grow up in my gum,
In a while the gap would stop feeling strange,
I wouldn't notice the tooth was gone,
The only reason I missed it now,
Was because it was there for so long,
Then slowly but surely over the weeks,
In the gap a new tooth grew,
And now it makes me wonder,
If people are like teeth too.

~e.h

My mother always told me,
No monster lived beneath my bed,
But she forgot to warn me,
It lay on top of it instead.

~e.h

Masked

A mask of every colour,
Every single shade and hue,
Built for just one purpose,
Built for hiding what is true,
A mask that hides the sorrow,
A mask that hides the pain,
A mask that stops the questions,
That keep nagging at their brains,
The special thing about this mask,
That sets it in its place,
Is that unlike all normal masks,
It never leaves my face.

~e.h

Roses

They say practice makes perfect,
And you've always been smart,
But you've got hating yourself,
Right down to an art,
It's now just a step,
In your morning routine,
To glance in the mirror,
And not like what you've seen,
The voice in your head lies,
But it won't let you know,
You gave up on ignoring it,
A long time ago,
Flowers in a vase,
Keep guard by your bed,
Yet you still see their beauty,
Though their petals are dead,
If they were a person,
They'd hate themselves too,
But they would always be loved,
By someone like you,
Although your petals are wilted,
And you think no one knows,
You're only counting your thorns,
While the world sees your rose.

~e.h

A Poem for Society

You told her if she wore that dress,
She'd be the prettiest of all,
You told her she should wear high heels,
Because she needed to be tall,
You told her how to cut her hair,
And how much skin to show,
You told her exactly what to wear,
"Trust me, because I know",
You told her if she wanted boys,
She had to change her ways,
You told her to wear make-up,
Because plain skin's not okay,
You told her who she could love,
That anything different was wrong,
But you made her feel secluded,
Like she would never belong,
She hated wearing dresses,
And she couldn't walk in heels,
She couldn't live to your standards,
And all of your ideals,
So you told her what she felt,
Was the furthest from the truth,
She couldn't be 'depressed',
Because she was in her youth,
You told her she was a 'freak',
That she never would fit in,
But then you told her nothing,

As she pressed a blade up to her skin,
And once she had decided,
That you would tell her nothing more,
You wish you'd told the truth,
As she collapsed onto the floor,
She didn't need the make-up,
That just being her was fine,
She could wear what made her happy,
That she could not be defined.
Then when you came to realise,
That she never knew you cared,
You wish that you'd have told her
The world was better with her there.

~e.h

She torments every thought I have,
Drowns my mind with words of terror,
But when I got to knock them from her mouth,
All my fist finds is the mirror.

~e.h

Run

Let's run away together,
Away from city lights,
Where no one knows our names yet,
And we can see the stars at night,
We'll camp out in the open,
Warming cold skin by the five,
Tell each other hopes and dreams,
And all of our desires,
We'll own nothing more than we need,
Watch sunrises colour the sky,
Learn what we're really here for,
Away from society's eyes,
This journey will be scary,
But we'll leave without a plan,
And I know that it will be all right,
As long as you're holding my hand.

~e.h

Seaside

Leave your worries by the shoreline,
And run your bare feet through the sand,
Let the water be a soft bed,
When you cannot hear to stand,
Make friends with flying seagulls,
And hold the sun up on your palm,
Before you duck beneath the water,
Where the world is mute and calm,
Tell the fish all of your problems,
As they all come swimming past,
When your lungs are close to bursting,
Swim above the waves and gasp,
Let the water hold your sadness,
And wash it right out to the sea,
So like a message in a bottle,
All your worries are set free,
And the sea might make you feel alone,
But the world has troubles too,
For how else do you suppose,
That the ocean got so blue?

~e.h

Empty Spaces

If there's empty spaces in your heart,
They'll make you think it's wrong,
Like having empty spaces,
Means you never can be strong,
But I've learnt that all these spaces,
Means there's room enough to grow,
And the people that once filled them,
Were always meant to be let go,
And all these empty spaces,
Create a strange sort of pull,
That attract so many people,
You wouldn't meet if they were full,
So if you're made of empty spaces,
Don't ever think it's wrong,
Because maybe they're just empty,
Until the right person comes along.

~e.h

I wake up in the afternoon,
And I sleep through my alarms,
But I would be a morning person,
If I could wake up in your arms.

~e.h

Sadness

They say that happiness will find you,
But I think sadness finds you too,
It sneaks up on you in darkness,
Just when you think you've made it through,
It opens holes in what was solid ground,
The kind you never know are there,
Until you go to take another step,
And find you're standing over air,
The world around you passes by,
In blurs of colour and sound,
Nothing around you making sense,
As you continue your plummet down,
You can't remember how it started,
And you don't know when it will end,
But you know that you'd give anything,
To stand up on your feet again,
Sadness is that feeling,
When the falling doesn't stop,
And it saps your life of meaning,
And all the good things that you've got,
So when you finally hit rock bottom,
And you look back up at the sky,
What you once had seems so far away,
The only thing left to do is cry,
People all yell out "save yourself",
Calling things about "happiness" and "hope",
But they're too busy with their lives to realise,
It'd be a lot quicker if they let down a rope.

~e.h

Sticks and Stones

Sticks and stones may break my bones,
But words will hurt much more,
They make me afraid to be myself,
Lift my eyes up off the floor,
Sticks and stones may make my cry,
But words will leave me cold,
Never again believing,
The nice things that I'm told,
Sticks and stones may leave me bruises,
But words will leave me scars,
As I lock myself in the bathroom,
With a blade pressed to my arm,
Sticks and stones may make me ache,
But words will make me want to die,
To stop my time upon this earth,
And kiss the ground goodbye,
Sticks and stones may break my bones,
But words will leave me numb,
And the only ones to think otherwise,
Are the ones behind the gun.

~e.h

The Wading Pool

She'd learnt to keep a shallow mind,
So people didn't have to swim,
And it led them all to think they knew,
The thoughts she held within,
But below the wading pool she'd made,
Was a world left unexplored,
An ocean of her feelings,
Hidden under the pool's floor,
The waters turned to blackness,
Where not even she had dared to go,
Stretching from behind her eyes,
To the ends of all her toes,
She didn't want to dive right down,
And find what lay hidden there,
Because she knew with all deep water,
Came a deadly lack of air,
But she didn't foresee the lonely boy,
Who found a crack in her cement,
Broke free of her wading pool,
And into the darkness he went,
He told her not to fear her thoughts,
As he took her by the hand,
And swum with her to places,
That their lungs could not withstand,
In their newfound love they both forgot,
The importance of their breath,
And interwoven in the world they'd found,
They both drowned in its depths.

~e.h

This life is but a garden bed,
The rain it comes and goes,
But you can prick yourself on all the thorns,
Or you can learn to love the rose.

~e.h

She & He: Part I

Her alarm goes off beside her,
A rough start to a rough day,
She pulls on the first clothes she sees,
And continues on her way,
The women on the sidewalk,
Seem to have life all worked out,
They don't feel the sadness she does,
And her own self-conscious doubt,
She's never been called pretty,
And she feels like she knows why
As she watches all the clouds,
Making patterns in the sky,
She doesn't want attention,
So she glances to the ground,
As though it may hold the answers,
That she's longing to have found,
Her day's like all the others,
Filled with voices in her head,
Telling her she'll be alone,
Until the day she's dead,
She walks back home defeated,
Her bed so big that she feels small,
Hoping that tomorrow,
She does not wake up at all.

She & He: Part II

He wakes to the warm sunlight,
But a cold and empty bed,
And thoughts of love he'd long to have,
Come back into his head,
The women on the sidewalk,
They don't even catch his eye,
Until he sees one lost in thought,
Staring off into the sky,
He's never seen such beauty,
But he knows she's unaware,
By the way she casts her eyes down,
And pretends she isn't there,
He knows too well the feeling,
Of thinking you're alone,
And he wishes he could tell her,
It's a feeling he has known,
His day's like all the others,
But it doesn't feel the same,
He just can't shake the lonely girl,
From staying in his brain,
He goes back home excited,
With a wondrous plan of his,
That tomorrow he will tell her,
How beautiful she really is.

~e.h

Somebody

Each day's filled with the absence,
Of the words you cry at night,
And I wonder what would happen,
If you let them out into the light,
Tell the world all of the lyrics,
Of the songs you haven't sung,
And the stories that you trapped,
When you learnt to bite your tongue,
Speak words you've left unspoken,
Out of fear that you were wrong,
Raise your voice so we can hear you,
You've been silent for too long,
The world appears so broken,
And although it's made you cry,
You know that hope is never lost,
So you've always wondered why,
Somebody doesn't fix things,
When there's so much they can do,
But I think it's time to realise,
That the 'somebody' is you.

~e.h

Talent

This world is filled with options,
So much to do so much to be,
Yet everyone has something,
Everyone but me,
I'm not the type for playing sports,
And I've never learnt to sing,
I'm always last picked for the team,
Not good at anything,
I'll always be a second choice,
Not quite enough for first,
I'd give up almost anything,
For the roles to be reversed,
To have just one thing in this world,
Where I find my passions lie,
Sometimes it seems so out of reach,
That I'd rather just not try,
I know it's out there somewhere,
That my talent does exist,
And I'm only getting closer,
With each new cross upon my list.

~e_h

These walls and floors and windows,
That we used to call a home,
Are nothing but a prison cell,
When I'm in this house alone.

~e.h

The Thing About Sadness

The thing about pain,
Is it won't last forever,
And it kills you right now,
But with time it gets better,
The thing about scars,
Is they all start to fade,
Until nothing is left,
Of the cuts that were made,
The thing about today,
Is there's always tomorrow,
And if you can't find your smile,
I have one you can borrow,
The thing about help,
Is beside you it stands,
But it won't know it's needed,
Unless you reach out your hand,
The thing about love,
Is you can't feel it's touch,
Until you let someone know,
That this world is too much.

~e.h

Universe

I stumbled across a grain of truth,
In the suns last drops of light,
As I stood out in my garden,
And watched the fruit bats daily flight,
They moved as though united,
Their flapping wings a silent dance,
And as they flew above me,
I stood frozen in a trance,
Their flight conveyed such beauty,
But had no thoughts of who would see,
And I wondered if they realised,
How much I wished that could be me,
Then as I looked I noticed,
That my life was a dance too,
And I was connected to the world,
In ways I never even knew,
The heartbeat of the planet,
Keeps a steady, even beat,
That echoes in the ribcage,
Of every creature that we meet,
I now know it's foolish thinking,
There's just one thing I can be,
Because I am the universe,
And the universe is me.

~e.h

View

The moment that you've been knocked down,
Is the moment that it counts,
And the moment that you've lost yourself,
Is the moment that you're found,
You can see the world much clearer,
When your eyes are filled with tears,
The only way to not be afraid,
Is to learn to face your fears,
You're not really afraid of the dark,
You're afraid of a lack of light,
And it's a fear of falling,
When you say you're scared of heights,
The only reason you know you're sad,
Is because you've been happy before,
You may say the world's an ugly place,
But you're only seeing the view from your door.

-e.h

I'm no Cinderella,
I'm just an average girl,
And the world might be my oyster,
But I am not its pearl.

~e.h

Gripped

One red line around each wrist,
Where your hands have rubbed them raw,
Why did I never notice,
How tight you clung to me before?
People think what made those lines,
Were handcuffs closed too tight,
And now that makes me wonder,
If in some ways they might be right.

~e.h

Trapped

I'm trapped inside a tower,
I've been locked and lost the key,
Now the darkness that creeps in at night,
Is my only company,
No one tries to save me here,
Since they can't hear my cries,
I pass my days in solitude,
Watch the world move on outside,
This tower isn't very grand,
It's really not that tall,
But still I can't escape it,
I can't break free at all,
You can't see this tower,
Just believe it's there instead,
Because my tower isn't made of stone,
It's all inside my head.

~e.h

Welcome To Society

Welcome to society,
We hope you enjoy your stay,
And please feel free to be yourself,
As long as it's in the right way,
Make sure you love your body,
Not too much or we'll tear you down,
We'll bully you for smiling,
And then wonder why you frown,
We'll tell you that you're worthless,
That you shouldn't make a sound,
And then cry with all the others,
As you're buried in the ground,
You can fall in love with anyone,
As long as it's who we choose,
And we'll let you have your opinions,
But please shape them to our views,
Welcome to society,
We promise that we won't deceive,
And one more rule now that you're here,
There's no way you can leave.

~e.h

I let my phone ring into silence,
Since I am not who they're looking for,
Although they might have the right number,
I'm not the right person anymore.

~e.h

This

When did we change,
From throwing paper planes,
And driving wooden trains,
To this.

And when did we grow,
From angels in the snow,
Lots of things we didn't know,
To this.

Can you put your finger on the day,
When we never again did play,
Our childhood wasted away,
To this.

And when did we get taller,
Our dreams get smaller,
So now the only thing that's left in life,
Is this.

~e.h

Breakdown

You're staring at the ceiling,
Trapped between these walls,
But you can't erase the feeling,
That you've been here before,
All the lies that they have told you,
Come crashing like a wave,
And as it drags you under,
You know you can't be saved,
If there's beauty in the breakdown,
You're the most beautiful of all,
But the higher people lift you up,
The harder you can fall,
The fear of what could happen,
Steals the light out of your eyes
In a world of broken people,
It's not hard to realise,
That though this world's still turning,
All your bridges are burning,
And there's nobody there by your side,
And though the lights shine bright,
They can't warm up the night,
And they can't wipe the tears from your eyes.

~e.h

Okay

I knew right from the very start,
You were a card from a different pack,
When I stared into your eyes,
And found you staring back,
You stole the air right from my lungs,
Like this world has stolen yours,
From the first words that you spoke to me,
I was already craving more,
We had our own infinity,
Crammed into a space of time,
And I hope you like the choice you made,
Because I know that I like mine,
This pain will always want to ache,
But I'll tell you that I'm grand,
And hope that you can't feel I'm not,
When you hold onto my hand,
I used to fear oblivion,
But now I no longer do,
Because I know if you're okay,
Then I'll be okay too.

-e.h

based on the novel "The Fault in Our Stars" by John Green

We live in a world,
Where we always want more,
But you can only be "rich",
If others are poor.

~e.h

Stars

You think you can define me,
That I'm a tick in just one box,
Like my being is a door,
That a single key unlocks,
But let me tell you something,
I have the universe inside,
I hold an untamed ocean,
With a constant changing tide,
I'm home to endless mountains,
With tips that touch the sky,
Flocks of grand migrating birds,
And deserts harsh and dry,
I house the wildest rivers,
And a host of sweeping plains,
I feel in waves of sunshine,
Or in unrelenting rains,
Don't tell me that you know me,
That "this right here is what you are",
I am the universe in motion,
For I was born from stars.

~e.h

The Writer

She bled unspoken words from her fingers,
Watched as they fell from the ends of her hands,
Until the paper beneath her was smothered,
In thoughts she could not understand,
The words danced with glee on the paper,
As they worked upon forming straight lines,
They'd escaped from the cage where she'd locked them,
And jumped free of her body's confines,
She couldn't stop them from telling her stories,
Couldn't hide them by biting her tongue,
So she watched with wide eyes as they shifted,
And each single sentence was strung,
They told stories she'd long since forgotten,
Swept into the dustiest parts of her mind,
And stories she'd worked to keep hidden,
Ones she prayed that nobody would find,
As she watched the word's dances get slower,
And then finally come to a rest,
She felt a smile creep over her features,
And a great weight lift off of her chest,
She'd thought that her words were all worthless,
But the paper left nowhere to hide,
And she finally noticed the beauty,
That she'd always kept bottled inside.

~e.h

Made in the USA
Lexington, KY
19 December 2017